Growing Up in
1940s War-Torn
England

JOYCE HOLGATE DEMILLE

an imprint of The Reader's Digest Association, Inc.

LifeRich Publishing books may be ordered through booksellers or by contacting:

LifeRich Publishing
1663 Liberty Drive
Bloomington, IN 47403
www.liferichpublishing.com
1 (888) 238-8637

ISBN: 978-1-4897-0026-1 (sc)
ISBN: 978-1-4897-0027-8 (e)

Library of Congress Control Number: 2013950827

Printed in the United States of America.

LifeRich Publishing rev. date: 10/18/2013

This story is dedicated to the memory of my sister, Beryl Dale, without whose loving help it could not have been written and to my daughter, Beryl, who gave me much needed assistance and encouraged me.

And also to my husband Cecil (Ces) D. DeMille.

Preface

I DECIDED TO WRITE THIS book after being asked why I fought the Germans, also because my daughter and others, after listening to some of my stories, suggested I write about them. I found that no one realized that seventeen-year old girls were drafted to work in the war effort, although we were never called veterans. It seemed to be a little known fact in the U.S. that England stood alone, with Hitler literally on our doorstep for some time so all hands were needed to keep them from occupying our little Island.

Acknowledgments

My first thanks must go to my sister, Beryl Dale, now deceased, who for many years reminisced with me from Yorkshire, England, over the telephone about the days we spent together during the bombing and then later at her little farm in the Cotswolds. She reminded me of the many humorous aspects of things we did together when I was able to visit her during the war.

This is to remember too, my cousin, Tom Davey, an intrepid Spitfire pilot, who with his girl friend, WAF Jill, also visited my sister when I could get a weekend off work in London. Many years later by which time I was married and lived in Georgia, we would visit on the telephone and talk about these times, and she would remind me of events I might have forgotten. So she also helped contribute to this book.

In later years I became friends with Dylys Clements, a lady with a great sense of humor and a good story teller. Over cups of English tea she reminded me many times of stories I had told her about living in London during the war and encouraged me to write these down in a book about those times.

Sandy Atkinson, without whose timeless help with the computer, I could never have finished the book.

I also wish to express thanks to my publishing associates at LifeRich Publishing, especially Emma Gliessman, whose patience with me was much appreciated.

But lastly, it was really my daughter, Beryl Westlake, who helped me the most with her very helpful critiques and advice about putting more of myself and other people into my writing, in other words to humanise the stories. She also helped me make my often stiff English language easier to understand for the American public. Besides all this she encouraged me daily to GET IT DONE.

Chapter I

"I have nothing to offer but blood, toil, tears, and sweat"
—said Churchill on May 10, 1940.

THE VERY WORD WAR CONJURES up vivid memories of World War II for
me. Should I begin when most people were praising the then Prime
Minister Chamberlain of Britain, who my father pronounced a silly old
woman, for his so-called peace talks with Chancellor Hitler of Germany?
How right he was! Yet, on hindsight this gave Britain time to prepare for
what was to come.

My brother, only 13 at the time, arrived home from Norway ahead of
schedule as the ship he sailed on was being chased by a German U-boat,
much to a small boy's excitement. This was in late August 1939, just before
war was declared.

The British Government issued an ultimatum to Germany that if
they attacked Poland, we would declare war. So on September 3, Prime
Minister Chamberlain gravely announced on the radio that we, with

France, were at war with Hitler's Germany. I well remember hearing this announcement while standing in our drawing room, looking out through the French doors at the sunny flower gardens outside, not really taking it in. If Hitler had invaded us then he might have succeeded in conquering us as no country could have been less prepared for war than Britain at that time. In the 6 o'clock news the King in his slow measured speech told us that we were once more at war with the German nation.

Men of all ages from 14 to 60, regardless of health, were drilling with garden tools. How grateful we were to President Roosevelt of the USA for sending supplies rather than entering the conflict at that time!

Rumors flew of attempted German landings at various coastal points which were off limits to the civilian population. Already German U-boats were chasing allied shipping crossing the North Sea to the British Isles. The Spitfires protected shipping in the English Channel. Gone were our annual summer seaside holidays at the south coast to which we would take the steam train with great excitement. I remember proudly telling my younger brother that the train would be travelling 60 miles an hour, never dreaming that one day I myself would be driving a car greater than that speed. What a different world it was then!

In later years I learned that Britain was struggling for survival but I doubt that thought ever entered my head in those days.

Both at school and at home we had been following the rise to power of the Reich in Austria, Hungary and Czechoslovakia in just one year. As I had pen friends in several countries at that time, I remember being very worried about what was happening to them and writing to try and find out. It wasn't until the end of the war that I realized my letters never reached them as they finally made their way back to me censored all over by the German Reich with "Return to Sender" stamped on the envelopes in German.

I remember being issued a gas mask with the injunction to carry it in its government issued buff-colored, cardboard box with string attached to hang over our shoulders, at all times. To me, as a schoolgirl this meant carrying it to school every day on my bicycle. All we, in my family, actually ever wore them for was when we sat around the kitchen table cutting up our garden shallots to make pickled onions.

However, only 16 at that time, it took the invasion of my beloved Norway on April 9, 1940, to really bring home the war to me. (I had spent a year there after an illness staying with family friends to regain my health.) The German army went into Norway by train through neutral Sweden. I'll never forget that day—still at school I cried all day. One of my teachers, seeking to comfort me, suggested that our annual end of term fund collection be taken up to help escapees arriving from Norway. The money, she said, I could present at the appropriate time and place. This I was proud to do when duly invited to a tea where we ate on real gold plates at the Guild Hall in London. The fall of Norway in May 1940 caused the downfall of Neville Chamberlain who was succeeded as Prime Minister by Winston Churchill, much to the joy of the Admiralty.

A little before this time, one day while riding my bike to school with friends I started gaily singing a little ditty, "Mrs. Simpsons got our King" (in 1936 our then King Edward VIII was dating a thrice-divorced American commoner, Mrs. Wally Simpson). Reaching a brow of a hill, suddenly with no thought of the consequences, I put my feet up on the handlebars. My pleated gymslip (like an American square-necked jumper with box pleats from shoulder to hem), showing no doubt a glimpse of navy blue bloomers and my head with panama-straw hat with band of school colors perched atop hair flying round my face, as I literally flew down that inviting hill. On reaching school, we filed into the assembly hall for our daily devotional. Were my cheeks red when after the hymn, the head Mistress said that it had been reported to her that a young lady from our school had been seen riding her bicycle with feet upon the handlebars. Miss Wallace then quietly stated that we were all to remain standing until the girl in question owned up to this most unladylike behavior. With Jean kicking my shins and Joan jolting me I had no recourse but to own up to it. For punishment my bike was confiscated for six months during which time I had to walk the hilly two and a half miles to school cum rain or shine. This was indeed a tough lesson.

Complete blackout was enforced by air-raid wardens who patrolled the streets at night and woe betide the smoker with a lighted cigarette in the streets. Darkness reigned supreme for the five years of war. My mother divided our heavy dark green winter drapes so that they could cover all the downstairs windows. I remember saying to her, "What a shame to have to shut out the twilight!" It was to me the calmest part of the day. Although our government had made available bales of dark material for the shops to order, there was never enough and my mother had to search all over London for the dwindling supply in order to cover the upstairs bedroom windows.

Very diligently we set about making sure we complied with all directives toward a complete blackout of our house. However, one Saturday a delegation knocked on the front door. It was led by the head warden of our street who very apologetically explained that these people, pointing to some ladies with him, had accused us of being spies. "Us spies!" I wanted to blurt out angrily but was stopped by a look from my father. My father invited them in and told them to look around. On entering the larder (a pantry), a step down from the back of the kitchen they pointed to a tiny window high up that had not been properly blacked out and then we all saw it. A tall red rose in the garden outside was being blown by the wind back and forth in front of that tiny window, looking for all the world like a signal to the sky. Our house stood in the middle of a U shape in the subdivision overlooking a farm and was thus visible to the whole neighborhood. "Well", one of the ladies said, "you can hardly blame us, you with all your foreign friends visiting back and forth before the war!" (This was highly unusual in pre-war suburbia.) Of course, my father went outside and cut down the poor offending rose—a real beauty my mother was glad to have in the house.

Note in my diary on July 14, 1940:

> *'PARIS FELL—Paris completely evacuated and Germans marched into the city. French army stopped hostilities by order of the government. Marshal Petain's government*

established to be friends with Hitler and give in to him in every way. Armistice to be signed between France and Germany. Germany to have all French coast, soldiers, airmen and planes, also whole fleet. However, later in July we captured greater part of French navy, unfortunately having to fight one submarine and a few destroyers.'

At the end of June came seven days of final exams in order to pass my school leaving certificate (matriculation). It was hard to study for these in the evenings when we were often called out to stirrup pump practices, etc. by our street warden. We also knew that we would not know the results of these exams until the September after leaving school (the custom in Britain in my days)—No graduation ceremonies for us.

Just before school broke up for the summer, a lone bomber broke through our balloon barrage and dropped a small bomb into the school's water supply resulting in it being contaminated with hordes of small frogs. (Anyway, that is what we heard at that time.) Whatever it was, many of us became sick and were lying up on the lawn in front of the school where a local doctor was sent for and he and a nurse treated us for extreme nausea. Later we learned we were now immune from typhoid fever. It was a beautiful sunny day so we all just laid out on the lawn until our parents came for us. After a two days rest at home we were able to return to school to take part in school-leaving ceremonies—no harm done.

Chapter II

"This was their finest hour…"

AFTER FRANCE SURRENDERED IN JUNE 1940 Britain stood alone fighting the war and Churchill said the following in his address on the British Broadcasting Company to rally Londoners: "This is the war of the unknown warriors; but let us strive without failing in faith or in duty, and the dark curse of Hitler will ever be lifted from our age…the whole fury and might of the enemy must very soon be turned on us. Hitler knows that he will have to break us in this island or lose the war….. Let us therefore so bear ourselves that, if the British Empire and its Commonwealth last a thousand years, men will say, 'This was their finest hour.'"

About August 8 of that year, late one afternoon, I was high up on a ladder painting the trim of our upstairs bedroom windows while my father was busy painting the lower windows at the back of the house. Suddenly I yelled out to my father excitedly exclaiming that a mock air battle was going on above us. "Get down off that ladder immediately!" my father called back to me, "that is no mock battle, it's a real one!" Thus began the famous air Battle of Britain. As I watched from the garden I saw German planes curling up, pouring forth smoke and flames as they fell to the ground while pilots bailed out in their parachutes. Fortunately they fell in the fields beyond our back garden (called yards in the States). The heavy German planes were no match for our fast little Spitfires which though fewer in number won the day. My father picked up a shovel and joined several neighbors who ran out to round up the pilots as they parachuted to the ground on the farmland behind our house. The German bombers were thus compelled to depart by our Spitfires and Hurricanes and this prompted Churchill's famous speech, "Never in the field of human conflict was so much owed by so many to so few." On the radio that evening we heard President Roosevelt say that America would give England all help short of war and Winston Churchill answered him, "Give us the tools and we will finish the job." The air Battle of Britain actually began that day in earnest.

"Our" first bomb was a landmine that landed by the fence at the bottom of our back yard, demolishing a pretty little fish pond, killing our 12-year old golden orf (a large goldfish). He was a family pet, grown so big we buried him in a shoe box, crying over his funeral as if he were human—our first casualty of the war. He had always come to us three children at the sound of our voices when we brought him food and seemingly seemed to enjoy being stroked along his shiny, golden back. A later bomb killed the Bantam chicks that helped ease our meager egg ration. Every day my mother would spend over an hour preparing our few scraps, left-overs, counting out proteins and carbohydrates in proper proportions to mix with half a cup of the daily allowance of meal to feed the hens. Mother also grew tomatoes, in what used to be a lawn, which we swore tasted of kippers as left-over kipper remains was their usual fertilizer. Kippers being our normal breakfast fare during the war. (For American readers kippers are specially smoked herrings, very salty.)

It was not long before silver, cylindrical "barrage" balloons began sprouting up round the outskirts of London. They were supposed to protect us from low-flying enemy planes.

Soon we heard the high-pitched whine of incendiary bombs over London, some of which fell on our own attic, but these latter we became adept in putting out. My father would grab the stirrup pump which stood in a bucket on the second floor landing directly beneath the attic, and with the help of my mother, sister and brother and myself passing along buckets of water from the nearby bathroom, we would quickly put out the flames. The broken roofing tiles we would pick up from the street and my father would climb up on a ladder and place them back in the morning. There was generally other debris to sweep up too. Windows which were blown out we replaced with sheets of wood. As we worked we would sing songs like, "Bless 'em all." "There'll always be an England," and "We'll hang out our washing on the Siegfried Line, if the Siegfried Line's still there."

It wasn't long before the government appealed by radio for men between the ages of 17 and 65, who were not already in the armed services, to volunteer as Local Defense Volunteers. Immediately thousands volunteered. These men were called the Home Guard. My father immediately joined them. He was a veteran of WW1 where as a small, slim young lieutenant of the King's Royal Rifle brigade he led a battalion of tough Welsh soldiers into battle in the desert. Knowing they probably doubted he could lead them, he decided he would march at the end of the line, having been warned that the Turks made a habit of catching and slitting the throat of the last man. On his guard he caught one of these Turks and instead of killing him told him he would be his batman, (shave him and take care of his uniform in the manner of English officers in those days). The man so admired his courage that he became a friend much to the astonishment of his men who felt sure that the man would slit his face while shaving him. Fortunately part of my father's school ROTC training gave him a little knowledge of men. Some years later at a chance meeting of one of these men we heard my father was much admired by them for his courage and leadership. I do know that later he was wounded—he showed us the holes in his thighs where a bullet had gone through one side and out the other and also said how when suffering from this he had a bad attack of malaria, and had been taken by some monks (who my father described as the poorest sect of monks in Salonica I think it was) who lived in caves where they took care of him until he was able to leave, meanwhile teaching him parts of the Bible in ancient Greek, much of which he remembered and tried to teach me.

The long arm of the law reached into every part of our lives. We were bombarded with directives on the radio and in our newspapers. We were advised to eat plenty of carrots to better help us see in the blackout. We were constantly urged by radio, newspaper and placards on local government buildings to 'Save bread and you save lives', and 'Serve potatoes and you serve the country', a poster issued by the Ministry of Food. Carrots and potatoes were grown easily in Britain and therefore plentiful. The government directed our lives in everything but we tolerated it all in order to achieve victory. As a footnote to this—my daughter still teases me as I often remind her that one potato has as much vitamin C as an orange. Not able to grow oranges in Britain and so unable to obtain them during wartime, this we were told to be the truth.

Mail was censored. There were no weather forecasts for fear of helping the enemy. Coastal areas were off limits, particularly in the south, so gone were our annual seaside holidays. We had 'Utility clothes and furniture,' very plain but practical and usually well made, but then only with ration stamps. Stringent food rationing commenced on January 8, 1940 and continued until 1954 by which time we were helping feed Germany. Gone were our usual plentiful supply of fresh fish from the English Channel, the whole coast round the British Isles was mined against the German U-boats, thus eliminating any foreign products from entering Britain. We were therefore totally dependent on what Britain could produce.

Rations per adult PER WEEK were: bacon, ham or meat—4 oz., sausages, offal not rationed but very, very scarce; one egg per week and one packet dried eggs every 4 weeks, butter 2 oz., cheese 2 oz., margarine

4 oz., milk 3 pints, dried skimmed milk—one packet every 4 weeks, sugar 8 oz., tea 2 oz., preserves one pound every 4 weeks, candy 12 oz. every 4 weeks. We also had a point system which gave us 16 points per month and this would buy one can of fish or 2 lbs. dried fruit. Babies had extra rations, such as concentrated orange juice, cod liver oil and milk. No cereals to be had in England at all.

Added to this, refugees began pouring in from countries taken over by the Nazis, including 30,000 Channel Islanders, evacuated Poles, French fishermen fleeing to Cornwall in tiny boats, and Norwegian whalers at sea after Norway was invaded. Fortunately, by then America was helping with their British War Relief, and we were able to get the occasional can of spam IF WE HAD ENOUGH POINTS AT THE END OF THE MONTH.

Here I should add that we greatly missed our Sunday dinner of roast leg of lamb as that would have weighed more than our family ration for five for meat. How my mother managed to feed us, a family of five, it is hard for me to conceive. I was in charge of making the mint sauce. I loved going into the garden to pick the green leaves, coming into the kitchen where I chopped them up, then put them into a mixture of warmed vinegar with a little sugar and let this sit out on the kitchen table until my mother was ready with the dinner. Like everyone where we lived our back garden was fenced in and had pretty green lawns and flower gardens with roses of many colors on trellis work made from tree branches. At the back of these we had our vegetable garden and rabbit hutches attached to the garden fence. We never sat in the front garden outside the house, only the back garden, our private domain, play area, and gathering place, to sit in the sun (if any) in the summer and entertain grandparents and/ or friends. It was always a pleasant place to be.

As soon as it got dark the bombing would begin and living on the outskirts of London many of the bombs that fell short of the city landed in our street. First came the smaller incendiaries which punctured the roof causing attic fires but did not do much damage as we were trained in the stirrup pump method of putting out fires. Also we took turns at fire watch duty. Although only 15 and 17 years of age, my sister and I took our 2-hour turns. I remember being woken up during the night to patrol our street wearing a tin helmet which I hated, as it was too big and heavy for me, but it was to protect us from falling shrapnel from our own anti-aircraft guns. In the evenings after supper, sitting round the fireplace we would work on making a large rug, each member of the family then at home taking a corner. Even my father, if he could get home from work at his bank in London in time to help, would be persuaded to make an attempt to knot a few stitches. This was great therapy for soothing our nerves during the noise of the bombing and/or ack-ack fire. Then we would talk about the ordinary events of our day. If it was a quiet night we would wonder where is Jerry tonight? My father would ask us how our school homework was progressing, telling us the importance of studying for our future. About this time he was upset to learn that my brother had no respect for his present female teachers. Here I should point out that in the England of my day girls were taught by unmarried female teachers at the local County School for Girls, while boys were taught by men teachers at the local County School for Boys some distance away, thus preventing any mixing of the sexes at school events. My brother apparently didn't see why he should bother to do homework for a bunch of ladies as the male teachers were drafted. Thus it was decided that he should be sent to boarding school for boys. Here I should add it was an old prestigious school, old in looks and repute where the discipline was hard in every facet of life. It is the saying that the leaders of Britain were made at schools like this. I may add that he has since told me that he hated it but he seems to have done well and excelled in sports as well as academics. Turning 16 years of age he decided he had had enough and applied to the British Tanker Co. to go to sea. Of course he lied about his age but as he was able to pass their stringent math test he was accepted. His life at sea was not easy but by the end of the war he was the youngest third mate in the company but spent most of the war in the Battle of the Atlantic, only landing once for repairs. His ship refueled ships in the Atlantic and often had to rescue sailors shipwrecked from torpedoed cargo ships, many of them being American ships, at some danger of course. We seldom had news of him.

Quoting from Ernie Pyle's book, 'Brave Men' in his chapter This England:

"I think that I was so afraid to hear the awful noise of those rocket guns that I was practically paralyzed. Finally they do go off. I guess I had expected too much, for they didn't horrify me half as much as I thought they would. The noise itself isn't so bad—it's what it sounds like that terrifies a person. For a rocket going up sounds like a bomb coming down. After I learned that and adjusted myself to it, rocket guns weren't bad."

—My note: He was alluding to the anti-aircraft fire.

Meanwhile I often wrote to my pen pal (who I had corresponded with since I was 11 years old) in California. I confided in her more about my school days than in anyone else. Her letters about her school days intrigued me. They were so full of interesting extra-curricular things not heard of at my school. It made my school life seem so humdrum by comparison.

Was I ever embarrassed began an excerpt in my 1940's diary—late in August when my sister and I were awoken by the whining noise of bombs falling and an intensely bright light penetrating even our very dark blackout curtains. We cautiously opened the bedroom windows and looked out on a ring of fire. It looked like our house was the only one of the triangle of houses that was not on fire. On hearing a commotion we ran downstairs to see what was happening. Neighbors were coming to our house to use our bathrooms, the only ones useable it seemed. My mother was in the kitchen busy pouring cups of tea, the ever consoling beverage of the British, while my sister and I went to reassure our dog who was shivering with fright. Mother gave me a tray to take to the new neighbors on the other side of the house who had not come to us. As I was just outside the front door about to go next door, the son whom I had admired from a distance and wanted to meet, suddenly appeared to take the tray from me. But before that could happen there was a loud crack as a sudden burst of our ack-ack (anti-aircraft) fire came crashing down on my tea tray, smashing the tea cups and dashing the tray from my hands. That it was fortunate that my head and hands were intact was not my first concern. Embarrassment hit me when I realized that I was wearing only my pyjamas with no robe, not expecting to be seen by other than family. Literally flew upstairs to my bedroom with a very red face while Bill retreated to find a broom. AND THAT IS WHERE MY DIARY ENDED FOR THAT DAY.

Notes In my diary are similar for each day:

140 German planes shot down this evening and so on—with air-raids most evenings.—Mother joined the WVS—Women's Volunteer Service. Another note in my diary said—couldn't sleep as searchlights and anti- aircraft fire making a terrific noise, explosions and German planes overhead all the time. Getting used to it after a while. One evening went to see a girl friend and while walking home after supper with her there was a terrific explosion so I ran home after the air-raid sirens went. That night the air-raid lasted 7 hours so we slept on the floor downstairs, but next day my sister and I sunbathed in the garden. Next day we had seven raids in 24 hours and I slept through two of them. 75 enemy planes down.

Already since the war started we had had air-aids every day. But work and school went on as usual. On a Saturday my sister, a girlfriend and I went into the countryside on our bikes, cycling with baskets on our handlebars, and picked blackberries. On the way we saw houses destroyed by incendiary bombs and cycled home slowly in a raid. Worst raid so far, on August 15, 16 bombs fell in little Carshalton where we lived, bombs at my brother's school and the east-end of London and the docks that resulted in 400 civilians killed and 1400 wounded in London alone. The next evening while walking with a girlfriend we watched planes firing on one another above, 7 Jerries and 3 of ours came down with wings bent up and pilots dropping by parachute.

Exciting note in my diary!

> received a telegram from Sweden telling us that our friends in Denmark were OK and so far, also our friends in Norway.

On September 7, 1940 the assault of the London Docks began. It was very frightening because the fires could be seen for many miles. We could see it all from our front windows. The whole sky was lit up, red with the fire of the fast falling bombs. We watched with mesmerized awe, wondering whether this could soon envelop all of London, even the outlying suburbs where we lived. Hitler thought we would lose the will to go on but on the BBC that night Mr. Churchill was determined that we "would not go under the monstrous tyranny of Nazism." "Here, here" was our response!

The bombing of the docks gave our exhausted pilots a much-needed respite. Their airfields and aircraft had been destroyed by enemy fire, also many pilots and by the end of September, the RAF were on the verge of collapse.

By the fall of 1940 armed with my School Certificate (Matriculation) with 6 honors, I was ready to go to work. All thought of college was out of the question as I knew that now 17, conscription was the rule and I would be called by the government to work wherever they needed me. Was not averse to this as, like all young people at that time, I wanted to be "in it", in my vanity believing that my doing my part was the only way the war could be won.—And that's another phase of my life in wartime Britain. Here I would like to add that I never saw any of my school mates again as the call-up (draft) had scattered us all.

Chapter III

"Remember, we shall never stop, never weary, and
never give in …" This was Churchill's broadcast to the
French to rally their resistance to the Nazis.

Many nights my sister and I would lie awake and listen to 'our' squadron of Hurricane fighter planes from Croydon, a nearby air base, flying high above our house on their way to attack the German bombers as they raided the convoys of ships bringing supplies to Britain. We would count them going and coming back to make sure that all twelve planes returned home. 'Our' squadron was led by the fearless Wing Commander Baden who had already lost a leg fighting the Huns over France. We felt we knew him although we had never met him and we prayed that he would return home safe.

Anticipating being called-up soon (drafted, that is) I decided to get some business education and enrolled in a school of shorthand and typing in a nearby town. The school was run by a strict spinster lady who tolerated no tardiness. This proved difficult for me as I had to take a train to get there but as it was a country town nearby I never thought this might prove a problem. However, the train was often delayed in starting from up the line and after a few days of tardiness I was told to leave as this was not to be tolerated for any excuse. However I had learned the rudiments of how to place my fingers on the typewriter and a few outlines of shorthand. So, armed with the books I had bought I decided to continue the lessons by myself, with the help of a friend to dictate to me. My friend, Sheila and I took our Welsh Sheepdog for a walk in the "oaks", an avenue of Stately oaks once part of a country estate, not far from where we lived, every evening after supper while the evenings were still light. One night I picked up speed forgetting that Sheila had been coughing lately and was therefore completely horrified when she started coughing up blood. So we then walked slowly home to her house where I told her mother what had happened. In a few days her mother told me that Sheila had had to be put in a sanatorium where she took me to see her. Sheila had always insisted on sleeping in a damp bomb shelter every night, being so scared of the bombing and I feel that probably caused the TB but she must have had a weakness already. I spent as much time as I could with Sheila and was with her when she died much to the dismay of my mother. This was my first experience of death and devastated me for a while. Of course, I blamed Hitler for it and cursed him loudly, childish I guess but my feelings at that time and I had to yell at something. We had been childhood school friends for many years and I missed her very much.

An excerpt from my diary on September 26, 1940, a few days later:

BLITZ KRIEG WHAT!!!—1 ½ ton landmine fell about 10:15 p.m. at the bottom of our garden, it was dropped by parachute. I was in the bathroom upstairs. Ceilings fell so we gathered in our kitchen. The dog was scared. Somehow staircase still there, kitchen habitable. All worked for 13 hours without a break, hammering heard everywhere.

7 houses flat, only 2 dead. My sister injured slightly by a piece of flying glass. House full of glass from broken windows. Over 1,000 houses affected. We escaped through broken windows in order to try and sweep up outside. "Jerries" were after 2 nearby airdromes. -

One thing I'll never forget, my father, mother, sister and brother and myself, while staring at the damage to the china cabinet with all the broken china and glass, my mother suddenly gave a little cry of joy saying, "now I can get all new stuff and get rid of all this dark mahogany furniture." I was so surprised all I could say was, "but what about our nice ginger-beer glasses?" Strange what pops into your mind at such a time. "Just be happy," my father interjected, "We are all safe, alive, who cares about anything else."

The next day while we were still working hard to clean up people started coming to see what had happened. They were curious, I know, but a nuisance; in the way. No one offered to help so we surmised they came from some distance. Bad news sure travels fast, we said. We had to go to work in the following days and without adequate security, looters were able to get it. I lost all my little girl jewelry among which was a little gold cross on a chain given to me by my Uncle, my godfather, when I was born and dearly cherished by me.

Not long after this a bomb pierced our bedroom roof and my sister and I could hear the warden calling for us. We tried to answer but still half asleep we found our mouths so stuffed with ceiling plaster that only muffled sounds could be made. Imagine their wrath when the wardens pounded upstairs to find us until they realized what had happened. After this, we were told, we were to sleep downstairs under the heavy dining-room table which, of course, we had no intention of doing.

Still awaiting the call-up letter I decided at my father's instigation to apply for work at the prestigious Bank of England, not at all sure that I would succeed. I was accepted and eagerly read the directives. The next day, overawed, I looked up at the imposing front of the building, the most important bank in the city, lovingly nicknamed "The Old Lady of Threadneedle Street". How could such an important portal of finance come to be known by such a homely name, I thought. Well, I can't stop outside dreaming about a name, I mused. I must pluck up courage and go inside those magnificent bronze doors. Having taken the first step, the next was to find the person I was to work for. I was glad I had taken the precaution to dress as the letter had stated in plain English: 'navy blue, black or very dark grey are the only colours which may be worn in the offices. If collars are worn they must be white. During the summer white blouses are allowed but they must be absolutely white without coloured pattern or design upon them.' This was only one of the long lists of 'Rules and Orders for Temporary Women Clerks', sent to me in the letter of directives. Upon arrival I was also told that it was expected that I would keep my hair above my collar and wear a hat and white gloves to work and to lunch. Later, I wondered whether these stringent rules and regulations could be kept when strict clothes rationing became the order of the day.

I was 17 and it was the fall of 1940 when England stood alone against the might of the German Nazis. I would not be able to join the ranks of permanent clerks because this was to be a stop-gap while awaiting my call-up letter from the government. I was ready for the call, eager to be doing what I thought of as "real war work." University (although I had earned a place in the University of London) was not a consideration at that time. Inside, my Supervisor, as the strict angular looking elderly clerk was called, told me I was to be a 'runner' in order to get to know the lay of the offices in the large, spacious, elegant old building. I was told I would be the 'runner' in the basement where important foreign banking chiefs who had escaped from German occupied countries had their plush offices and where soft red carpeting cushioned the corridors. This intrigued me and delighted me, as it meant action instead of sitting endlessly at a desk. But this was to come later I found. Meanwhile I soon found out that the name 'runner' was a misnomer. Actual running was not permitted, nor was whistling. I was delighted to find that one of the offices on my route was the domain of a prominent Scandinavian banker but I dared to not show my knowledge of his language as I had been warned that I was to be seen when handing him mail but not heard. But this did add some interest to my job. One day as I gaily whistled on my way, the austere supervisor suddenly appeared and with grim-set mouth scolded me for my indecorous behavior. Fortunately for me a tall Norwegian banker opened his door at that time and said in excellent English, "It's nice to hear a cheerful sound down here in this dungeon." At that, without thinking, I said in Norwegian, "Tusen takk" (thank you), much to his surprise. Later I heard that he had inquired after me.

After a few weeks of this pleasant duty came the command to take a seat at a long table with many other clerks, where silence reigned the day long. The image of that long table would remain with me until my dying day, I thought. They were male and female clerks, all intent on this various paper shuffling. As I had a smattering of several languages I was given batch after batch of bonds, stocks and shares from which I was to take out any that might have owners in enemy countries. All eyes were to be glued to this endless stream of papers, hour after hour, day after day and there was to be no talking to the person sitting next to you. In fact I never knew the names of any of my cohorts there. Ten minutes were allowed to go to the rest room, which was so far away it didn't leave much time for the necessities.

Much as I revered the elegant old building and the prestige which went with working there, great was my relief upon receiving my call-up (draft) papers. It was not everyone who was afforded such a privilege of working in this bank, I had been told several times, whenever I took too long going to the rest room or stayed a minute over the allotted hour for lunch.

All in all, this phase of my life lasted about six months, after which I excitedly waited to find out what His Majesty King George VI's government had in store for me. Sometime later one evening, much to my surprise, my father brought the Norwegian banker home for supper and then I learned that they were old pre-war friends.

Another excerpt from my diary a little later:

> *A crowd was forming—what is it all about, I thought. General Eisenhower was being given the key to the City of London and it was during MY lunch-hour. How fortunate—I was there hoping to see this event. How exciting to have the chance to see this great leader of our combined armies but how was I going to be able to see him? Much too short to be able to see over the crowd, I swarmed up a lamp post, complete with white gloves and navy blue suit of the secretary of those days. Never did I dream that one day I would live in, and learn to love the small town in South Georgia that would become "Ike's" favorite golfing resort.*

Commuting to work during this time for me was by train. Walking from the train station in the evening after work during the winter months was often quite hazardous when the fog was thick. I would feel along the fences of the stately old houses as I walked down the road, counting them, to find out where I would have to cross the street to my road on the other side of the highway. The train station was a ten minute walk uphill from our road on a street called Beeches Avenue. (The tall beech trees formed a golden arch across the street, a beautiful sight in the fall with the bright gold and red colors of the leaves.) Although only about 17 miles from London from where we lived as the crow flies, it took about an hour or more to get to the city. The train I normally took to work ended at London Bridge which meant I had to walk across the old London Bridge to my office in the "city" of London. The bridge was always packed with people walking across and we would often wonder why one lone bomber (which we sometimes heard flying above us) did not bomb the bridge and thus kill many people. But visibility was generally very poor owing to our perpetual morning fog and, as we learned later, unlike our allied planes, they didn't have radar to see through the low-flying clouds and fog. Young as my friends and I were and sure of our invincibility, we would joyfully point skywards, saying "Ha, ha, Jerry, you can't see us through our London fog!"

I was young enough to want to stay in town after work some evenings, in spite of the nightly bombing. My father told me emphatically NOT to take the last train home.

Spending an evening in town after work my date and I missed the train I should have caught so he put me on the last train while he went back to his barracks. Look for a 'Ladies Only' carriage, my father had said. This I did but in the strict blackout was unable to see that it was occupied and sat down on the lap of a Canadian soldier. Then I realized that all of the seats were occupied by Canadian soldiers returning to their barracks after a night in town. Later I correctly surmised they were stationed in old houses in a neighboring town next to the small town where I lived, a pretty quiet suburb. There were no corridors on commuter trains so it was impossible to find another carriage. Then the "fun" began, but not for me as I was terrified of Canadian soldiers and they tossed me from one lap to another with much mirth. After a while, they asked me not unkindly how it was that such a little girl was traveling alone late at night. I told them proudly that I was 17 and had just been drafted to work as a secretary in a war department. In disbelief, but more kindly, they asked me whose lap I would prefer to sit on for the rest of the journey. My fears somewhat dispelled, I realized that though slightly inebriated, they didn't mean me any harm.

The end of the line came at Sutton, about 2 ½ miles from my home. This last train did not go any further so I knew I would have to walk the rest of the way home in the darkened streets, a hilly walk and I was tired but it was my own fault. One of the soldiers wanted to accompany me, saying that I was too small to walk the rest of the way home by myself in the dark. Then, my fear returning, I started to run and didn't stop until I got home, knowing also that my father would be waiting up for me, probably with a good scolding.

Then came a three-day holiday so I took the train to Balham, a suburb of London, to spend time with my grandparents. My grandfather had had the front door of their house painted white. It was a town house situated at the head of a street at right angles to one opposite. My grandmother said that made their house easy to see by the Jerries when they flew over the neighborhood at night. "How ridiculous" was my grandfather's answer to her—"How could a German pilot spot our house from so high in the sky?" "Well, we are told they can see a lighted cigarette" was her answer. That weekend, while I was there it happened! A huge bomb was dropped in their back yard, in the middle of my grandfather's rose bed, his pride and joy. The air-raid warden immediately arrived to tell us to leave the house at once as the bomb had not yet exploded. While he and my grandfather were talking and thus distracted, my grandmother made the most of the opportunity to go back into the kitchen, winking at me not to say anything. She came back triumphantly carrying a saucepan of prunes she had managed to snatch off the stove. For that she was reprimanded by the warden. Smiling, she reminded him that even prunes were rationed and anyway as they were still cooking on the gas stove a fire could have caused the bomb to blow up in our faces. Quick thinking on her part, I couldn't help thinking. After that we all left by train to stay at my parent's house until their bomb could be detonated.

The next excerpt from my diary mentioned:

> 'ship carrying children being evacuated to Canada torpedoed—all children drowned. Terrible! Poor kids, they might have been safer in the London blitz, bad as it was.'

Chapter IV

FINALLY THE LONG-AWAITED CALL-UP LETTER arrived. However, there was no glamour job for me. The government took one look at my diminutive height and weight (4 ft. 11 and 89 lbs) and decided it had to be a desk job without a uniform for me. The letter told me to report to the War Office, Ministry of Fortifications and Works Shipping Department. My spirits perked up when I was told to meet with a certain Captain Blood at the Engineers Department of Shipping and Bomb disposal. My arrival at the right office (always confusing to me in a city) was hastened somewhat by the sudden blast of a nearby bomb. In my fear of being late for an important appointment, I had disregarded the air-raid warden's whistle to take cover in the nearest shelter. However, the blast whirled me into a basement which happened to be the war office shelter where my new boss had just arrived. And so began my first war job! Interesting work, calculating the space in the holds of merchant ships to carry ammunition to soldiers fighting overseas. Plenty to do in an office in an old building heated only by a fireplace. It was hard to get there on time as the commuter trains were often bombed. I always had my knitting with me but often the train was so crowded I had to stand. Looking out of the compartment window I could see many of the houses on the way were damaged by bombs but the people still obviously living in them. Here I must interject that at that young age I was noticing any young male traveler not yet called-up (drafted) into the Army. Having attended a girl's school I had no boy friends—all those I knew in my street had already joined the Air Force and had been lost in the Air Battle of Britain. My diary digressed many times to mention that I had seen some young man on the train that I would like to meet but I knew I probably never would see him again. In my new job I had to work all day Saturdays, the normal rule at this stage of the war. With Sunday school the norm on Sundays, all girls, there was not much time to meet new people. The young soldiers in my adjacent office were engaged in very dangerous work every day, detonating bombs that had not yet exploded, so my fellow workers told me.

Not yet 18 years of age I was allowed to leave the office early before the nightly bombing began in earnest. However it being slightly misty a lone bomber had penetrated into that part of London early one night as I walked towards Victoria Station to catch my train into Surrey where we lived. Suddenly the air-raid siren sounded, a huge bomb just blew me across the highway, landing me high up on a spiked fence outside an office building. Suddenly, an angry air-raid warden yelled at me, "What are you doing climbing that high iron railing when an air-raid is in progress? Why aren't you in that shelter on the other side of the street under that eh, eh…" building, he was about to say when he saw that it was no longer there, just a huge cavity where the large building with the shelter in the basement had been. Many workers were killed there. Then he turned his attention to me as I was clamoring to be helped down –"why are you up there!" he exclaimed in irritation. Mad as hell, I asked him how did he think I got up there by myself, hurting as I was held up there by the iron spike through the collar of my dress and I was afraid I would soon be undressed and was a long fall to the pavement. Needless to say I was as surprised as he was. How did I get there then? The only reason we could think of was because my body was half-turned to cross the highway and the subsequent blast of the bomb had blown me up there. Once down on the pavement my reaction was to throw up and then I walked to the station where my train had arrived. I sat in a 'Ladies Only' carriage and got out my knitting to soothe my nerves as I was all alone there and the hum of a German bomber could be heard above, so the train did not depart for a while. Sitting there I realized that the collar of my coat was torn and worried that my mother would notice and ask how it happened. I quickly took it off before going into the living room as she would undoubtedly have been so upset she would have asked my father to try and get me away from having to commute to London to work in the war effort. I knew I could mend the tear before she saw it again. Walking into my office the next morning I was surprised by the sudden rush to hug my neck. My co-workers thought I had died in that air-raid shelter which they had seen still smoking the next morning and knew that people had been buried alive there under the ruined office building. Well, my Uncle had always called me the Survivor when as a baby very premature they kept me alive in a shoe box on the stove.

That same night there was a heavy raid on the city of Coventry with over 1,000 casualties and the Cathedral was bombed flat. All those dead were civilians. The Houses of Parliament in London were damaged and Buckingham Palace, but our Royals never moved out. That evening in the news we heard that Hungary had joined the Axis.

The next day, the Lance Corporal assigned to our office for the week, escorted eight of us girls to the Strand Lyons Corner House brassierie in the evening to protect us, he said, and entertained us by saluting to all the generals we passed, thus causing them to have to salute him back—what a nerve we thought!

Meanwhile the Germans were pouring into the small country of Norway by way of train through Sweden. The Norwegian government forces in Norway were defeated by the overwhelmingly larger contingent of German manpower and were forced to flee to Britain, finally arriving with their King Haaken in London. Once situated they needed personnel and word was sent out that anyone with any knowledge or skills in the Norwegian language were in demand and asked to apply for work. Naturally I answered the call with my ability to type, and write Norwegian. It excited me that perhaps now I could help the war effort in a more important way. My present office was delighted to let me go to hopefully a more interesting job for me. However it proved far harder and really above my expertise although as it proved a very good learning experience for me. In my innocence, I was far too young in my knowledge of life. My boss was the Naval Officer in charge of Norwegian Navy personnel. Imagine the shock of typing his dictations containing sexual words to do with men's health problems I had never heard of.

Also, it was my first experience of typing from the Dictaphone which consisted of a wax cylinder that didn't give a very clear sound of the words. At the end of the dictation I would have to rub it off and leave the next layer of wax for the next dictation. So it behooved me to listen very carefully and turn the cylinder back to make sure I had the words correctly before rubbing it off. Unfortunately, I made the mistake of asking one beautiful but not very kind Norwegian Navy girl to help me about a word. What a blunder that was! The sailors heard of my innocence and the harassment I received made me tearfully ask the boss for help. He answered by asking me whether my mother had ever given me a book to read (about sex) or told me anything. I had to answer in the negative so he told me to go home and find one and read it.

We worked every Saturday morning. I had met a Norwegian girl in the office who had lived in England most of her life so we became friends. One beautiful Saturday afternoon, glad to have a few hours to ourselves she suggested we take off into the countryside outside London. So we decided to ride our bikes toward the coast, knowing full well that the seaside towns were off limits. That we were not in uniform made

it worse. It should be noted that owing to my diminutive size I was never put in uniform but was told I was their mascot and given a sailor suit to wear in parades, to my embarrassment. But on this trip we were just two carefree teens tired of so many wartime restrictions and decided to ride as far as we could. Suddenly appearing from behind a huge pile of potash, a military policeman accosted us wanting to know what we thought we were doing in a restricted area. My friend, a big blond Norwegian girl made them more suspicious than I did, not daring to say a word. I escaped from German officiousness she said. This answer did not sit well with the policeman. "Rank" he said first, then "Where do you girls work? The name of your bosses, etc. and why are you riding bicycles in this restricted zone?" I let Hilda do all the talking with her attractive Norwegian accent but even so we were asked how we would like to spend time in the small jail there while they checked up on us. By now I wasn't too happy, knowing that it would be easy for them to fire me as I did not have to live in the barracks in uniform with all the Norwegian girls. Anyway, as luck would have it, after a few telephone calls we were allowed to go free with the admonition to remember in future that the whole coastal area of England was off-limits to civilians and most military not having the necessary paperwork in hand. But what would they say to us when we went to work on Monday? My friend was punished with restriction to barracks while I was transferred to the non-military shipping department in order to split us up and a better choice for someone as immature as I was at that time. It should be noted that in those days most English girls of our age, at least in the beginning of the war, were far more childish than today. The war probably made us grow up as we were drafted at the age of 17 from mostly girls' schools. At least that was the milieu I came from.

Chapter V

In a world broadcast from London in April 1941, Churchill said:
"When we face with a steady eye the difficulties which lie before us,
we may derive new confidence from remembering those we have
already overcome. Nothing that is happening now is comparable
in gravity with the dangers through which we passed last year."

WHENEVER CHURCHILL SPOKE TO ENCOURAGE us he would hold up two
fingers like a V (V for victory) and this became the symbol of the war.

The Norwegian Shipping Department was my final destination for
the rest of the war. The offices were in the more frequently bombed
financial district of London but a district I had always liked, in the
vicinity of the Tower of London and its park. The only uniforms were
those remnants worn by elderly Norwegian Sea captains who had
sailed their ships to England rather than return them to their occupied
country to be used by the Germans. This, of course, was a great help to
the war effort, England being an island very dependent on its fleet of

merchant ships. Most of the female clerks were typists, English with a few Norwegian women and our tasks were varied, some translations, but mostly letters and typing to do with shipping documents and filing of same. I was given the task of translating and listing the small tools in the engine departments of whaling ships with the help of photographs of the various types of nails, screwdrivers, etc. and became quite proficient in this, if I may say so myself. There was always a Norwegian ship's engineer or someone who could assist me when stuck for information. We would take turns in making the ever-brewing coffee for the men. One day I mistakenly decided to take the kettle home and boil it out to start the next day with a clean one—my mistake! What has someone done to our coffee kettle? The taste has gone! Apparently you never clean a Norwegian sailor's kettle.

Sometimes a Scottish girlfriend and I would take a sandwich for lunch and walk down to the park round the Tower of London to sit there and eat it. On the lighter side of the war—It was our lunch hour and my friend and I were taking a walk in the park when we saw two American GIs ahead of us. No, we weren't following them to flirt with them, too shy for that, but to satisfy our curiosity. "Let's walk behind them to see if they split their pants when they sit down on one of these park benches," we said while giggling. We were so unused to seeing men in such tight pants; our British Tommies wore baggy khaki pants.

Other times we would walk downtown to find out what we could get for lunch at one of the food shops, such as a bakery or tea shop. Now and again I was able to meet a cousin or two or girlfriend working in another office for such forage into town. I was always hungry, maybe because I was the youngest of my friends, and I remember gazing at some meat pies in an ABC shop when one of my friends teased me, saying "Look at Joyce, eyes on those meat pies, doesn't she know they are filled with cat meat, ha, ha!" "How can you say that?" I answered. Of course it was probably horse meat but undisturbed I would buy and enjoy one, thus assuaging my hunger. It must be explained here that my mother went without much of her rations in order for us to have enough for our sandwiches. My friends would prefer some of the sweeter baked goods when I hankered after meat. Having always had plenty of milk to drink before the war, it was hard on a teenager to have so little at breakfast before going to work. My friends could never understand why I stayed so tiny when I so eagerly ate those meat pies. It was a standard joke in London that the disappearance of so many cats in London was caused by them being killed for food but this was hardly probable. But it must be admitted that mice had become a nuisance in the old offices where files were often found chewed upon.

While I was commuting to work in London, my brother had decided to leave his hated boarding school and volunteer for the war effort. Although only then 16 years old he was able to pass the very difficult math exam to apply for apprenticeship in the prestigious British Tanker Corp. and so he was soon off to sea. He soon found that although training as a midshipman his duties to begin with were more arduous than those of the ordinary seaman, down in the hold, scraping paint, etc. But he grew to love the life at sea. He used to say that his old ship, built in the old way with rivets was stronger than the newer ships in the Atlantic where he stayed most of the time fueling merchant ships at sea, never coming into a port.

Meanwhile when I was called-up my sister was taking her school-leaving exams, ten days of them, sitting in the trenches they had helped to dig outside the school, most of the time with water up to her knees from the dampness ever prevalent. After she left school she went to work at a farm, her wish to work on the land for her war effort.

The strain of commuting to work in London when the trains were often bombed with the resultant necessity of getting off and walking until other transport could be found began to have a toll on me. After all, I was only 89 lbs and barely 4ft. 11 ins. tall. My mother took me to the doctor who said I was anemic. All drugs were sent to the service men overseas (except those needed for babies) so he told my mother to have me drink a cup of stout (a dark beer) (normally drunk by the elderly) every evening before going to bed. When she poured me a cup

full after one taste I grimaced and said, "I can't drink that nasty stuff."
She sighed and said, "Well, I guess I'll have to ask your father to try
and pull some strings to get you out of having to do this war work."
She knew that would make me change my mind and I drank that stuff
gladly every night.

From the next entry in my diary:

> *"Ouch, ouch." I said in a loud voice as the last two stitches
> were put in my appendices. This however I do not recollect
> happening but was told by my mother, years later. The
> lady doctor who was operating on me for appendicitis
> had started on the fourth floor of a large London hospital
> when an air-raid forced everyone to take the elevator
> down to the basement. She was left having to hold the
> two sides of the cut together before she could stitch them
> together, resulting in a rather ugly and wide scar. It was
> in the winter of 1941 when afternoon raids were the norm
> and in the moving the anesthesia had begun to wear off.
> This accounts for the somewhat unusual looking scar that
> has been frowned at by subsequent doctors, no doubt
> thinking that it was a botched affair.*

About this time it was brought to my attention that the old Norwegian
church at dockside was in need of Norwegian-speaking volunteers who
could help refugee Norwegian sailors bringing their ships to England.
Many of them needed help in writing to their families in Norway (by way
of the Red Cross). Naturally I volunteered but first my father insisted on
taking me there, fearing naturally that the docks were in the worse place
for the daily bombing. However, after taking me one Sunday morning
quite uneventfully, it was decided that I be allowed to take the train
every Sunday morning to east London to join in the service and stay
and help where I could. This I enjoyed, feeling greatly recompensed
by the pleasure it gave so many men and women I met there, some of
whom became life-long friends. With another volunteer job I was not so

fortunate. At London Bridge railway station there was a canteen for the troops getting off the train. It was situated at the corner of the station and London Bridge, making it a very noisy place during the bombing but I think it was probably the ack-ack firing making the most noise. Fortunately the bridge itself was never hit.

The swing music band of the Canadian band leader, Guy Lombardo and his Canadians played loudly most of the time. The stalwart woman in charge was watching me (I felt) thinking I wasn't strong enough for the job, I later realized, as the heavy stoneware cups and saucers made the trays very heavy indeed. Her misgivings were not unfounded. Unfortunately, when a soldier pinched me in the behind I dropped my tray, breaking everything on it. The harried, matron-like manager told me if I couldn't take a little teasing from the soldiers without dropping my tray, I didn't need to be working there. She needed strong, mature women who could take it. It was no use my explaining that it was the suddenness that made me drop everything. She fired me on the spot. At that time I was living with my grandparents so as not to have to commute so far. So they were glad I had been fired as they worried about my being out so late at night at such a strategic spot when nightly bombing was the norm.

The train I usually took to commute to London was too often delayed by bombing, resulting in my having to walk and then bus part of the way, scrambling over debris part of the way, resulting in my arriving late for work. It being late summer, I was told to take the "milk train" as it was called, leaving very early in the morning. My family decided I should stay with my grandparents where I could take the underground (tube) which would not only be quicker but safer.

"Where am I and how did I get here and how can I get out?" These were the thoughts that rushed into my mind. The evening started out normally enough, a quiet date with an elderly Norwegian friend known to my grandparents as someone I could safely be out with in London's blackout. But what happened later is still a bit hazy in my memory. It appears that I said goodbye to my friend in order to accept an invitation to a party given by a group of Red-Berets in the Norwegian Army. They took me with others in a jeep to a nightclub, I think it was. (Here it should be noted that naive as I was at that age I had no idea what a nightclub looked like.) The young men intrigued me as I knew they could be dropped over Norway next day, never to return if captured by the Nazi invaders there. So they painted the town red when in London for an evening. This should have warned me, but I was in need of some fun. What I had to drink I do not remember but probably ordered a gin and soda. I remember we sang and joked and I never even finished my small drink. But after that I remember nothing until being rudely awoken when my skirt was yanked down by a young man exclaiming loudly, "Fyfaen ……." Swearing, angrily in Norwegian to the effect that I was a … virgin! Now wide awake, I recognized the young man standing over me—well, thankfully my honor was saved by this son of a leading government minister. Losing interest in me he walked away. Then I looked around to see young women and men lying on the floor as I had been, all from the party of the night before. With daylight now streaming in through big windows on one side of the room, I realized we were in a large house and I must have been carried there by one of the young men. But how and why?

Had something been put in my drink? But first I must get away and think about that later.

I looked out of a partially open window and saw there was a fire-escape reaching down to the road many feet below. Then I knew we were in a room several floors up. Nothing daunted, I saw a milkman's van in the street below, so I decided I had to get down that long steep ladder. All this happened quicker than words can tell. I dared not look below as I hurriedly climbed down. On reaching the street, I asked the milkman the way to the nearest underground station. After he told me—wonderingly, I ran before he could ask me any questions. From the name of the tube station, I could see that it was somewhere in north London and I had to get to south London where my grandfather was no doubt worrying about me. I was hoping he had gone to bed thinking I had sneaked into the house but then I remembered I had no key and the windows would be shut. My grandfather scolded me and said I would have to promise to come straight home from work from then on—a hard promise to make for an eighteen year old.

Then came a humdrum few weeks of work and no play, with the usual trial of traveling home in the black-out, helping my grandmother with dinner and dishes and sitting quietly with my knitting during the evenings.

Chapter VI

IT CAME IN THE MAIL. Imagine the excitement I felt on getting a letter from Buckingham Palace requesting my presence in audience with King Haakon VII of Norway. What an honor for an eighteen year old girl to receive during World War II!

He would receive me, it said, at the Norwegian Embassy where he was living after having recently escaped from the Nazis in his beloved country which was invaded by the Germans on April 9, 1940.

After taking time off from work my Norwegian boss cautioned me not to tell a soul. There were too many spies, he said, around impressive buildings in London during the war, even though there would be nothing to denote that the Embassy would be named as such. Take a taxi, he said, to a short distance from the Embassy and walk the rest of the way to the building.

I had bought a smart summer hat (the only article of clothing not rationed) to go with my best light blue tailored suit for the occasion, so felt fitly attired for this momentous event in my young life. But how disappointing it was that I could not tell a soul. Who would not want to shout it to the world—look at me—I've been commanded to meet the King of Norway!

Private   6th August
                                    1943.

BUCKINGHAM PALACE.

Dear Madame.

I am desired by The King of Norway to thank you very much for sending on Miss Bull's kind good wishes for His Majesty's Birthday and for your own very kind thoughts of Norway. I am returning the letter to you as I feel that you will value it as expressing the wonderful spirit of those living under the invasion, so little

But why was I sent for you may be asking. Well, I had received a letter which had been smuggled out of Norway from my friends who were in the Norwegian underground. Presumably it had arrived in a fountain pen used in those days as it was tightly folded and written on rice paper so it could be quickly swallowed if discovered. But this I realized later. At the time I had found it under the roller in my typewriter from where it popped out when I started to type that morning. I knew better than to inquire as to how it came to be there. In the letter it asked me to send their best wishes to their king on his birthday the following week on August 3rd. This I had done and the King wished to congratulate me on getting messages through and for me to explain a few things in the letter known only to me and my friends.

I remember being ushered into the high ceilinged-room with its heavy doors and the King towering over me, a charming old gentleman. He put me at ease right away, speaking in his Danish-Norwegian so easy for me to understand. Explaining some of the place names in the letter, I told him they were using my pet names from the time when I was there as a child and not able to speak the language, as a code for drop off places for short-wave radios for the underground. These were to be used for allied airmen shot down over Norway so they could follow the news of the war and communicate with their headquarters in England. The King listened intently purposely not asking what kind of liaison I had with the underground, thinking no doubt that I probably could only guess at my connections, not wanting to put them into words.

After a few more minutes of friendly conversation about his beloved Norway, he suggested to my great surprise that we have lunch together. Thereupon he called his aide on the intercom to inquire whether he had an appointment for lunch as he would like to invite his young visitor to eat with him. However, he was informed that he had an urgent meeting with a senior military officer at that time. I'm so sorry he said to me—I would have enjoyed lunch with you.

While standing up to leave, this kindly old gentleman was striding to the massive door with its large white china door knob to open it for me, saying that it would not be easy for such a tiny young lady to open it. How I left and went back to work I can't even remember but I do know I was walking on air wondering whether it had all been a wonderful dream.

After France fell, the British Expeditionary Forces were trapped on the coast of France at Dunkirk. The British Navy could not help evacuate them being surrounded by the French navy. A fleet of small boats manned by ordinary people, anyone who had a boat of any description, set sail in a quiet armada for Dunkirk to bring back as many men as they could carry, a very hazardous task reaching the men in the turbulent waters of the English Channel while undergoing constant bombing from the German planes. However with the Royal Air Force fighter planes to protect them by keeping the German planes at bay the rescue continued for nine days. Around 300,000 troops were thus brought off the beaches of Dunkirk. We called this the "Miracle of Dunkirk" I later heard that an elderly Uncle of mine had skippered a lifeboat sailing back and forth carrying a cargo of troops many times before being blown up by a German plane.

When Churchill received the news of Hitler's invasion of Russia in June 1941 he made the following broadcast on the BBC: "We have but one aim and one irrevocable purpose. We are resolved to destroy Hitler and every vestige of the Nazi regime. From this nothing will deter us— nothing. We will never parley. We will never negotiate with Hitler or any of his gang. We shall fight him by land. We shall fight him by sea. We shall fight him in the air, until with God's help we had rid the earth of his shadow and liberate his people from his yoke."

A note in my diary at that time:

Have the Germans forgotten what happened to Napoleon when he tried to fight the Russians not so many years ago?

About this time there was a rumor, later proved correct, that Hitler's deputy, Rudolf Hess, had landed in Scotland, a mystery at that time but thought to be a peace offering, requesting that we join forces with the Germans in fighting the Russians. It was kept quiet by the Government in England but overseas rumors ran riot.

Lord "Haw-haw" as he was called by us, broadcast propaganda from Berlin every evening in English and told terrible lies about how the war was going on and how terrified the British had become. He probably knew better.

Chapter VII

"What kind of people do they think we are?" Churchill said in an
address to a joint session of Congress after Japan had attacked Pearl
Harbor on December 7, 1941. This brought thunderous waves of
applause for five minutes. Stirring all Americans with his faith he
said "that in the days to come the British and American peoples will
walk together side by side in majesty, in justice, and in peace."

UNLIKE MOST OF MY FRIENDS this came as no surprise to me as my father
had always said that it wouldn't be long before America would be attacked
by Japan and would enter the war. In those days bankers always knew
more about world affairs.

Quoting from James C. Humes' 'The Wit & Wisdom of Winston
Churchill' when a Canadian photographer snatched his cigar from the
prime minster it caught him in a disgruntled expression which was the
result of the most famous photograph of Churchill.

Here is a brief outline of events in the course of the war as noted in one of my diaries:

> '*End of August 1942 Rommel (the Desert Fox) and his Afrika Corps battled to open the road to Suez. They failed and fell back. In October-November the British 8th Army under General Montgomery attacked the German and Italian forces under Rommel at Alamein in North Africa and the enemy were driven back to Tunis. After this victory at Al Alamein, Churchill said at a Lord Mayor's luncheon in London: "We have a new experience—a victory—a remarkable and definite victory. No, this is not the end. It is not even the beginning of the end. But it is, perhaps, the end of the beginning."*'

After the Soviet Union had been invaded by Germany, the Germans had enough to occupy them on this other front and this gave us some reprieve from their attention to us in London. So I was able to return home probably to the relief of my grandparents. I had decided to attend an evening class in London after work before taking the train home. I had never really had any training in accounting. The classes were held in an ancient school building in the center of the city. Sitting at a desk next to me was a young Canadian who soon asked me out to eat at a local restaurant after class. Our friendship was just starting to blossom when spasmodic bombing affected our classroom lights. The bulbs were lit by gas so any bomb in the vicinity would blow them out and the class would have to stop. This put an end to my desire to continue returning to the classroom.

In November 1943, the Big Three (Churchill, Stalin and Roosevelt) at a meeting in Tehran, decided that the British-American invasion of France should take place in the spring of 1944.

Meanwhile I was still commuting to the Norwegian Shipping office in London where I came in contact with Norwegian seamen who were escaping from the Germans in Norway and seeking to join allied ships in England. Much of my work had been in translating the engineering logs of a whaling ship which taught me (from photos of the parts) knowledge hardly useful for my future. One day the Captain in charge of my department asked me to help him buy some lace curtains for his wife, promising me in return a steak lunch in Soho. This was too good for me to refuse as firstly Soho was off limits to a young woman like myself and the thought of steak unheard of in those days was something I will never forget. At my age I really didn't know much about lace curtains or where we could find them but felt that probably in Soho anything could be found. I hope his wife was satisfied with what we found when he finally was able to smuggle them to her. That was the only steak I had in all the years of the war, a never forgotten treat!

A date standing out in my memory was May 3, 1944 when my mother told me to invite a few friends to supper to celebrate my 21st birthday, which in those days meant the coming of age. No big celebrations were planned in those war years. Fortunately, Stanley, a favorite cousin was on leave from the Army at that time and so able to come to my little party and that was the last time I saw him. He was the life of my little party with his wit and charm. Only 18 years old he had been posted to the Center Pool of Artistes who were on their way to entertain the troops when a bomb hit their transportation killing them all outright. The newspaper report said his death had robbed the stage of a brilliant young actor. He had studied at the Royal Academy of Dramatic Art and played with a known repertory company touring the British Isles before joining the armed forces. His death was such a loss to anyone who knew him and upset me very much.

One night a bomb hit our house resulting in the ceiling in the bedroom I shared with my sister falling on us. It was early in the morning and we woke up feeling stifled with the stuff all over our heads. The local air-raid warden came into the house to check on us, yelling upstairs to ask if we were OK. We tried to answer them but only muffled sounds came out, even our mouths being stuffed with the powdery white stuff. So we ran downstairs as they scolded us for not answering until they saw our predicament. This was when they decided that my sister and I should sleep downstairs. But that didn't last long—we both missed our comfortable beds.

That summer much of England suffered the "baby blitz" when German bombers attacked England in retaliation for the heavy bombing strikes against Germany. About then a Scottish girlfriend of mine married to a Norwegian working in the office with her invited me to go to Scotland with them to visit her family in Edinburgh, for a week to give me a reprieve from the bombing. That was indeed a wonderful break for me, the one and only time I visited Scotland. I saw Loch Lomond and Glasgow on the other side of the coast. Unfortunately both friends are dead now.

On June 6, D-Day—called Operation OVERLORD started by the combined British and American forces, comprising naval and air force and ground troops, lead by U.S. General Eisenhower and our General Montgomery. Allied air power made it possible to land paratroopes in France behind the German coastal defenses. The French underground soon joined in the struggle to free France by generally sabotaging German installations. The German army surrendered on June 27 but they had destroyed the port of Charbourg in France and much equipment there. This hindered the continuation of the war in Europe.

On June 10, 1944—I was standing on the lawn in our back garden when amazed I saw this strange- looking thing flying overhead spitting flames. At first sight I couldn't believe my eyes, thinking it was something out of science fiction. That evening on the radio news program I learned it was the first flying bomb to reach London. The V-1 nicknamed "buzz bombs", or "Doodlebugs" by us. They were small pilotless planes, rocket shaped, like a blimp with fins which flew low, making a loud noise and a

*great blast when they landed or hit anything, altogether
terrifying but at least we would generally see them before
they landed. We got so used to them that many times
while gardening, we would stand and watch them fly
over us, wondering where they were going to land and
what damage they would do. We knew that as long as we
could see them they were not likely to hit us. These, then
were Hitler's secret weapons we had heard were to come.
London was the target and Hitler thought this final terror
would make us want to give in.*

A month later, on July 12, I telephoned my parents to wish them a
happy 23rd wedding anniversary when they asked me what that terrific
noise was. At that moment a buzz bomb (rocket bomb) hit a neighboring
house. It was the worst day of bombing from the pilot-less planes. I
counted 14 flying over our house resulting in a terrific barrage from our
anti-aircraft guns, shaking the house all night. My parents were staying
at my sister's little farm house that weekend and my father asked if I
needed him back in our house in Carshalton Beeches immediately. I
told him no, I was fine. (However, inside I was feeling scared and glad
to spend the night with a friend.) I knew he needed that short vacation
away from London with my mother. This was the worst day of bombing
over London of the V-1's.

The V-2 bombs came in early August. They were much larger and
far more deadly, being rockets which were shot into the air at a great
height and not heard until they exploded. Very destructive and terrifying,
they flew four times the speed of sound. Both the V-1's and V-2's were sent
from bases in German-occupied France against London and Southern
England where we lived. There was no warning possible because no
one could predict where they would land. These, then were Hitler's
secret weapons we had heard were to come. Hitler had hoped we would
insist on peace in order to escape from further attacks from these deadly
weapons, but that never occurred to us.

I remember vividly one day at the office the walls of which were huge glass panes separated by pieces of steel. A V-2 rocket bomb exploded some distance away and yet near enough to cause our office to shudder at which my boss yelled to us to get under our heavy metal desks. But, with the invincibility of youth, I just HAD to finish typing a sentence, barely missing having my fingers shattered by a steel bar which fell on my typewriter a hairbreadth from them. My boss had no need to tell me that should teach me to obey him. Needless to say, I was understandably appalled when later in the States; I was to learn of the recognition accorded the German so hated in Britain for his invention of the rockets, Werner von Braun.

When the Allied ground armies in Normandy overran most of the German rocket bases in France and Belgium, the Germans continued to launch rockets from bases in Holland. Together the V-1 and the V-2 bombs killed thousands in south England (mostly London) and seriously injured many more in the nine months of this blitz and 4 out of 5 houses were badly damaged.

The following is an account of my worst experience in WWII—My heart literally jumped as the commuter train stopped at my home station when I saw the rubble on the platform on the other side. While clambering over the debris, I was scared thinking that my mother who was to return from visiting my sister in the country might be on that train. It was pointless to find out where that bombed train came from so I ran the short distance to our house where the windows had been blown out (nothing surprising about that) but the telephone just inside was ringing. I reached in and grabbed it only to hear, "Where have you been—why don't you answer? We have a lady by the name of Mrs. Holgate here—please come and get her." "Where is that?" I answered, full of fear. "At Croydon Hospital where we have no space to keep her."

Without a thought as to how I could reach that hospital some 15 miles away and knowing that no trains would be going, I ran down the hill to see if there was a bus I could take at least part of the way. I found that I would have to get to the next little town for that so ran harder than I knew I could the next three miles, where I found a tram to take me the next two or three miles, then another bus and so on until almost breathless I reached the hospital. No need to enter it and ask for my mother—there she was sitting in a chair outside the entrance. She was in a daze rather than scared as she sat with most of her hair cut away and bleeding scars mostly round her mouth. Somehow or other, I can hardly remember how, upset as I was to see my mother like that, I managed to get a taxi to take her home. She managed to tell me she had the money in the large purse she always carried for she knew I probably would not have enough for that. There were no bank cards or visas in those days.

She said little on the journey home except to say she would like a good cup of tea. I felt she was in shock and didn't want to ask questions. But she did tell me there were so many injured worse than she was and so no one had time to give her a cup of tea—most unusual in those days (the usual comfort medicine in such circumstances).

I found that she had had a head full of small chips of glass from the carriage windows, many in her mouth, accounting for the numerous small bandages. How long she had sat there outside the hospital I had no idea.

At that time we had started to sleep downstairs under the dining room table, having been ordered to do so by the local air-raid warden. The upstairs bedroom ceilings and windows had been bombed. I helped mother on to our makeshift bed and she asked me to help her undress, saying that something was pricking into her back through her vest (a silk or thin knitted garment we wore over our bras in those days). "Oh, Mum," I said, "you were in a Ladies Only carriage." "How do you know?" she answered. Then I showed her a large shard of glass which had gone through her old-fashioned corset, down the whole length of her back, with the large words printed in red on it announcing LADIES ONLY. What a miracle it did no further damage!

The next few days are no longer very clear but I do know that my father came home by train that weekend and took us down to the country cottage where my sister was preparing to live. Without time to allow my mother to recover from any shock, we all started pulling old newspaper off the walls inside the old cottage walls in order to be able to paint them and make the place livable. I do remember my mother's hair grew back completely white.

My parents were helping my sister to buy the small cottage to keep her little farm going because if left uninhabited evacuees arriving on the scene would take possession of it and at that time possession was nine-tenths of the law. Before my parents left again to go into the country they moved the furniture that was useable (Most of the furniture looked diamond studded from bits of glass blown into it and thus unusable.) from the house while I stayed behind to supervise the rest of the removal. What upset me the most was seeing my secretary desk where I did my homework and kept my favorite books ruined by shattered glass and desk part scarred with glass embedded in the wood. Two days later a huge bomb dropped three doors away and the rest of the house was reduced to a shaking, cracked shell. Fortunately for me I was sleeping with some friends in the next road where just a ceiling fell on me. Getting all the powdery stuff out of my thick hair and mouth I couldn't wait to get back to my house to find my clothes. Meanwhile I was alone trying to keep up our home in Surrey and commuting to London to work. The doodle-bugs were in full swing at that time and the house was once more blasted. With so many windows out and no one to help me patch them up as I had to be at work on time—no excuse permitted—it was no surprise to find that burglars had looted when I came home from work. Not much appeared to have been taken but not one cupboard had been left undisturbed. In fact the contents of every room were heaped together in the center of each room. However, the most important things were stolen—all our coupons for food and clothing were gone. There were so many forms to be completed and government officials to overcome that it took literally months before new coupons could be obtained. In my exasperation I wrote a very touching (or so I thought) story to the Ministry of Health telling them how ill I was getting because I was not able to buy a new pair of shoes to keep the rain out.

Chapter VIII

MEANWHILE, DORIS, MY AMERICAN PEN pal had asked me if there was anything I would like her to send me. I replied that I would love to have a piece of cotton material to make myself a summer dress as even with coupons, cotton was not available in England. So she wrote back asking me for my measurements in order to figure out how much material to send me. My reply giving her my measurements was rejected by the British Post Office and sent back to me with a curt notice that it was against Defence Regulations to ask for gifts from the USA. The following is a copy of my reply to the G.P.O., London.

13th July, 1944
Your Ref. B5431
G.P.O. London

Dear Sir, Rejected letter to Mrs. D...

I am sending this letter and trust that you will see your way to forwarding it at the Government's expence in postage.

The objection you raise is absurd when the facts are known. I have corresponded with this lady for many years and she has recently asked me to choose between a dress and material. This gift is entirely unsolicited and I cannot ignore the offer without doing a grave discourtesy to one with whom I am on affectionate terms.

The matter is all the more stupid because if I had not mentioned my measurements the lady will doubtless obtain them (or a rough estimate of them) from a mutual friend in the U.S. Army over here at the moment.

I would mention that I am not entirely uninformed on the Defence Regulations as I worked in the Bank of England for a while in their Exchange Department. Moreover my father is the author of a work on this subject and he assures me that I have in no way contravened any existing law or Order.

Yours faithfully,
(sgd.)
JOYCE HOLGATE

Fortunately my letter was finally sent to Doris and she sent me enough material to make my dress. What would I have done without such a good friend as I had lost all my coupons during the bombing? I only hope I let her know how much I appreciated her kindness.

The weekend after that (managing to get the Saturday off work for a change) I took the train to Shipton-under-Wychwood in the Cotswolds (west of London). From there I walked along a country lane to my sister's little cottage. Asking my sister what I could do to help she handed me a bucket and told me I could milk one of her goats as I probably needed the milk—she knew how scarce milk was in London except for babies. "Stand astride the little goat," she said, "and then she won't be able to kick you." Well, after a few attempts I finally managed to squirt some milk into my pail and was very glad to be able to drink it. My sister was concerned at my thinness and said she wanted to fatten me up with farm produce that never seemed to get to London.

A cousin, an intrepid pilot in the Royal Air Force, would sometimes visit my sister and mother at the little smallholding (it could hardly be called a farm although that is what we liked to call it) and sometimes I would bring a Norwegian friend and then Jill, a WAAF friend of my cousins too for a carefree weekend away from London and the bombing. These few weekends were prized and full of fun as a rule. We all tried to ride my sister's huge carthorse, only to fall off to much laughter from us all. But believe it or not, my sister could make him jump over hedges and even competed in a local horse event, much to the surprise of the local gentry, to see a small girl in milk covered jodhpurs on the broad back of a huge carthorse which she handled as if he were a thoroughbred. My sister had only to whisper in his ear to get him to do anything for her. This reminds me of the time when she asked a few of us if we would like to lead a bull back to the neighbour she had borrowed him from to service her cow. She handed us a heavy dangerous looking chain attached to the bull's collar and thought the three of us could take him across the country road. Easy, thought we! But not so, that stubborn bull refused to budge, hard as we all pulled. So finally my sister walked up to his ear and whispered something and then she led the docile bull back to his home. She certainly had a way with animals.

After a delightful weekend with good country food and entertainment it was time to go back to town and work.

Chapter IX

"Twice in my lifetime the long arm of destiny has reached across the ocean and involved the entire life of the United States in a deadly struggle … the price of greatness is responsibility …The people of the United States cannot escape world responsibility … We have now reached a point in the journey where … it must be world anarchy or world order."

THESE WORDS WERE TAKEN FROM a speech by Mr. Churchill in August 1943 when after a meeting with President Roosevelt he went to Harvard University to receive an honorary degree.

Notes from my diary of August 4, 1944 when staying with friends.

The bomb fell about 2:30 a.m. on Thursday morning. That one was the first one I heard but apparently a great many bombers had been flying over all night dropping bombs indiscriminately. The ceiling on Tony's room behind me fell down waking me up. Nothing could be done until it got light, but we could see one of the houses or what was left of it on fire. I think the bomb fell in the Tucker's garden— Mr. and Mrs. Tucker who were upstairs in bed were killed. Mr. Pike was the first to find them—they were just in pulp. (his description) So you can see that house is condemned. We were up early then so Mr. Quick came straight home with me and helped me get my cabin -trunk and a box of stuff I had hidden in the cupboard under the stairs, as it remained intact. No ceilings, no doors, no windows, walls cracked, etc. but in spite of many battens broken on the roof about a dozen tiles were still left on. The frame-work of the French-doors and windows is like small pieces of fire-wood.

Mrs. Pike was injured by falling down in their damaged house so Mr. Pike took her to the hospital. Little ten-year old Richard was a brick—he insisted on helping me sweep up some of my rubbish. I thought it best to help where help was most needed so after helping the Quick's a little went round to the Pikes where Richard and I set to work on their house. We were offered WVS HELP BUT I SENT THEM TO OTHER HOUSES BUT one of the women found little Richard's leg bleeding from several cuts which he hadn't even noticed and bound him up, much to his disgust. He really worked hard all day. It was funny when he pulled the lavatory chain and the water fell down on us in the kitchen. We couldn't help laughing in spite of the mess. The Warden came round telling everyone to go to Ruskin Hall for a meal but I went back to the Quick's. Sweeping up and shovelling up glass had given me such a headache that I took a couple of aspirins and was asleep before I realized it. I had even taken their gas oven to pieces, washing it and put it back together again.

In the fall of 1944 my father came to Carshalton Beeches to check on me. He decided it was too dangerous for me to continue trying to live in the shell our house had become so decided I had to go back to staying with my grandparents in London from where I could take the tube to work. Although loathe to leave our house I decided it would be nice to sleep in a bed again instead of under the dining room table so I acquiesced if my grandparents would have me. Of course, they welcomed me with open arms.

January 1945 turned unusually cold, even for England with snow falling for several days. Rocket bombs were falling, at least 12 a day at that time. It was still sad to me to see so many people sleeping on the platforms of the underground stations when I went to work now using the tube train again. This way it was easier for me to get to work on time with less fear of being in an above ground commuting train where bombing was still a possibility. Rationing became more acute, lower amounts in many foods, even bread was now rationed.

Meanwhile battles were ranging fiercely over Europe with thousands of men being killed in action until finally Germany surrendered on May 7, 1945—Victory in Europe—NORWAY FREE.—Two days holiday—people milling round Pall Mall and the Royal Palace, waving flags, crowds of joyful people everywhere. Bonfires on the common, floodlighting that night in town after years of blackout. My Norwegian friend and I attended the Norwegian dockside church to give thanks for the end of the war in Europe.

Listening to the news on BBC radio we learned of the meeting of Churchill, Roosevelt and Stalin (known as the Big Three) in Yalta, in the Soviet Union. The end of the war then in sight these three leaders met to agree on plans for occupying Germany. However Churchill never trusted Stalin. Unfortunately President Roosevelt, a close friend of Churchill, died shortly after this and Harry Truman became President of the United States. Churchill said President Roosevelt was the greatest friend Britain ever had.

Before the end of the war letters started to arrive from old family friends in Norway and Denmark. What a relief to find that many old friends had come through alive.

Quoting from my friend who was like a sister to me:

'First I want to tell you we have not doubted one single hour how it will end. We do not have much to eat—it is fish, but what fish—we would never have eaten it in peace time. But the food situation is not the worst. The worst is that we cannot say or do what we want. Even if you only smile in the wrong places you are put to prison. We cannot even wear the clothes we chose. If you wear a red cap you will get to a place you do not like My boy friend -(her future husband—my note) has been in prison camp Grini for 13 months and in these days he will be sent somewhere else, we do not know where and think that most of our boys are going to be sent now .- (my note—we later learned that allied forces liberated these men the day before they were to be sent to concentration camps in Germany).- As you understand these are all our best boys. Last week was one of my other boy friends killed. The Germans shot him straight down because he tried to get away and he really did get away but by chance they saw him and killed him. He took the risk I expect because he did not dare to be caught. He probably thought he could not stand the torture and therefore he would rather die than talk. He was only 26. I'm afraid it often happens but we do not always hear about it. My mother's friend is widow and both her boys are in prison.—(My note—the oldest one was a childhood friend of mine Who I had been thinking of and who I finally was taken to see him in a rehabilitation hospital recovering from torture he had received in an infamous Nazi Concentration camp, Belsen-Belsen I'll never forget seeing him with his unseeing eyes in a bent up old body and face of a very old man He could barely walk with a cane as he hobbled along the dusty path towards us.)—' Now they have started National work—it is not more national than the quislings. I will never join it. (My note: quisling was the name given to the Norwegian Nazis) They can rather put me in prison for the rest of the war. I do not think it will last much longer now. --- Thank God it is soon summer. We have never before had such a beautiful spring as this year and never so early. It is so lovely with sunshine and light green trees and grass, that you almost forget the war, but then you see a German soldier or a quisling and then you remember. If you were in Oslo now you would think it was a German town. You hear German spoken everywhere and see them both with uniform and without. We can never go anywhere.—Everywhere you meet them.. I never thought we could hate anybody as we hate the Germans and quislings. But now they have lived their days and soon it is our turn and then....Do you know we have not seen my boy friend more than twice in 13 months, and now we have not seen him for half a year, and he has been allowed to write once in the same period. At Xmas we were allowed to send him a packet of 2 kilos, but we were not allowed to write to him nor was he allowed to write to us. (After the war they told me he never even received

the parcel so we presumed the German guards got it.) I think you
know a bit about how we have it here, if you could send us a word
of how you are it would be nice. Please send our love to our king
and tell him we all are waiting for his return. Give our love to all
our family from all here. Much love from Vesla.' (My note: Vesla
is a common nickname in Norway so could not easily to traced.)

After reading that letter I remember crying that night and having
many nightmares afterwards, thinking about friends I had known in
Norway.

Many other similar letters began to arrive from friends in Norway
and Denmark, and other liberated countries in Europe, one even from a
friend in Neuchatel, Switzerland, expressing the hope that we (my family)
were OK and offering their congratulations for the victory of the war.

Here is a translation of another letter received from the younger sister
of Vesla who wrote the above letter. Kirsten writes: 'It was very strange
and nice to hear from you after so many years. You can guess that we
have had a lot of trouble the while the occupation lasted. You can bet we
have often been nervous. You can bet there was great celebrating in Oslo
on the 7th May. You know that the news doesn't come until 6:30 but at
5:30 everybody knew it. I was at school at the time. I embraced not less
than two mistresses that day. We didn't get much done that lesson, you
can bet. All my class wept. You know that when the first English troops
came everybody had been lined up for many hours beforehand. When
they came they were bombarded with flowers. They had their laps full of
flowers. People shouted and shrieked as if they were mad. These troops
were something different from the Germans who paraded the streets.
These were well behaved nice people. They looked nice and kind, as they
are. Just opposite to the Germans. What awful necks they had, fat porky
necks. Brutal like no others in the world. You ought to know how they
treated our boys. A friend of ours (Lillemor, Vesla and me) was taken
up to Victoria Terrace (the Gestapo Headquarters). There they beat him
almost to death. Then they threw him down into a cellar, damp and

cold. There they left him lying for two days and nights. Afterward they took him up to a red-hot furnace room where he could hardly breathe and made him stand right next to the furnace fire. Then they tied him to a chair and fixed his arms with thumbscrews. He had just had an operation on his knees so they put one there too. When he asked "Why don't you shoot me instead of torturing me to death?" They hit him in the face with a knuckle-duster. He had no feeling left in this arms and legs for many days afterward. Now he is free again. You know that Truls and Klaus have been in concentration camp. Truls is in the home-front (underground army) and Klaus also.—I work as a "Lotte" for the home-front, Lillemor and Vesla also.'

I found out later that Vesla had been very active in the underground army, finding German ammunition caches, destroying them in the fjord, hiding shot-down allied pilots and feeding them and supplying them with radios, etc. ending up with a huge sum of money on her for her capture.

Chapter X

With the end of the war the Norwegian Shipping Department began to break up as the Norwegians were anxious to return to Norway and rejoin their beleaguered families there. I was offered and accepted a job in the Norwegian Department of the BBC Overseas news department called 'This is London' broadcasting in 46 languages from offices below ground to offer news around the world. This proved most interesting as I worked as secretary in the Norwegian Department meeting many Norwegians joining. I was sent out to do interviews which were translated into Norwegian for broadcast to Norway, firstly to the underground while Norway was still occupied. Some of them when translated by the Norwegian news reader didn't seem to make sense and often those written by me in Norwegian made me wonder whether I was forgetting how to write the language until I realized that sometimes words were altered to hide a code telling where a radio or package was being dropped to help someone in hiding from the Germans. Our news service was very valuable to occupied peoples all over the world and we still hear from people who thank us. We even had a Children's Hour to which my sister sent several stories which I helped translate. My only claim to fame on the air was to crunch a carrot in one of the stories! All this was broadcast many floors underground of course.

In this job I met many celebrities. Mrs. Eleanor Roosevelt came one day with a short message written out to the Norwegians. She asked me to translate it and read it to the Norwegians. On perusing, I told her it would be better if she would read it to them herself, telling her that they would understand it and be delighted to hear her talk to them. She was a delightful person to talk to with a smile that lit up the world. I was invited to a Garden Party at the Palace (as a reporter) and I remember being asked to tie the sash of the Queen's Lady- in-Waiting standing next to the Queen while introductions were being made. How I happened to be right there I can't remember and being left handed at tying bows I dare to think how that turned out. Also I remember that I was competing against the London Evening News paper reporter for our BBC program so rushed to reach the telephone before he did. All this dressed up in my new garden party hat to look like an invited guest.

August 15, VJ Day:

> *Peace at last Three days holiday. My aunt and I with my Norwegian boy friend went to town to see the King and Queen in their open carriage open the parliament and later my friend lifted me up to see the Royal family on the balcony of Buckingham Palace. The next day my brother, John arrived complete in his uniform of a Third Mate in The British Tanker Company, the youngest Third Mate on record so we were justly proud of him. He had served all through the Battle of the Atlantic fueling ships at sea hardly ever seeing land. That evening went to a dance in Piccadilly where I was proud to be escorted by my brother.*

END OF WAR TIME DIARIES.

Although relieved that war was finally over it left me feeling restless. Of course, I was glad that the killing was over. I had come through it all and realized that I had grown in many ways and gained strength feeling able to cope with anything that life threw at me. But what did life hold for me now? I missed the many Norwegian friends I had made during these years. But mainly I needed to go back to Norway to revisit old friends to find out how they were after the pressures of the German Occupation. I also had a sense of freedom, being able to leave London completely and go, go, go somewhere else. I had nothing to worry about and could be my own person, able to enjoy whatever life had to offer a young woman, maybe go to a dance, and be with young people no longer at war.

Epilogue

IN GERMANY AFTER THE WAR, while working in the translation department of the Kreditanstalt fur Wiederaufbau (The Reconstruction Loan Department), then under the direction of my father in the American Zone of Germany, I met a girl called Ruth. She much admired my father and the work he was doing to put Germany back on her feet. She wished me to understand why they (the German people in general) thought so much of Hitler. She said, "What if you grew up thinking that your nation was despised and even hated after the humiliation of the Treaty of Versailles after the first world war and then came a man who made you feel like a great nation again, who gave you pride again. This is what Hitler did for us. After the defeat of the British Army at Dunkirk we were assured by the Press, that any day we would be landing in England and we trusted in Hitler to bring this about any day." I liked Ruth very much and felt her genuine pride and disbelief in what her rulers had done to the Jewish people, as well as other countries they had invaded. She was from Prussia and blamed the Russians who had invaded her former state in North Germany, then called the Russian Zone, for many of the cruelties going on there.

This conversation occurred after the following event when I had registered some disgust. Coming back after lunch to the small office we shared, I found the three girls drinking champagne and eating cream cakes to which they invited me to partake. But first I asked them what they were celebrating. They answered that it was the anniversary of Hitler's birthday, to which I turned heel and left while laying on the table a book I had just received from Norway with a picture on the cover of a Norwegian being tortured by a German SS man. Needless to say I didn't return to the office that day.

Glossary of English Words

Ack-Ack	anti-aircraft fire
Aerodrome	small airport, such as Croydon
Call-up	draft
Garden	yard
Gymslip	everyday school uniform
Huns	Germans
Jerry	Germans
Kippers	smoked herrings
Lavatory	toilet
Soho	area of East London
Tommies	British soldiers
Tube	London underground trains
WAAF	Women's Auxiliary Air Force
WVS	Women's Voluntary Service

Bibliography

Authors diaries from 1940 through 1945.

'The Wit and Wisdom of Winston Churchill' by James C. Humes

About the Author

JOYCE HOLGATE DEMILLE was born in London, England in May 1923. Educated, in England, Norway and summer school in Neuchatel, Switzerland. According to FSU, matriculation from high school in London, England at age 16 was equivalent to 2 or more years of college in the USA. At age 17 drafted to work in London at war office, commuting from suburbs, secretary in department of Norwegian Navy, Norwegian Shipping Department, and later BBC Overseas Department, beamed to underground workers in Norway, until the end of the war. Went to Norway to see how old friends had fared under occupation and worked as a secretary in the British Embassy in Oslo, where she was invited to help entertain the celebrated English Philosopher, Sir Bertrand Russell, on his visit to Norway. When stress from commuting during bombing finally caught up with her, she left to spend time with parents in Frankfurt-am-Main, Germany, where her father had been sent by the World Bank to help reconstruct the German economy. Worked in The Reconstruction Loan Corporation (run by her father, Dr. H.C. F. Holgate) as a translator for a while. Met her husband, Cecil (Ces) D. DeMille, a sergeant in the

US Air Force who made her laugh again. Married Ces in Shipton-under-Wychwood, in the Cotswold Hills in England on October 6, 1951. They arrived in Georgia September 1952 where she worked as a Legal secretary in Valdosta, Georgia. Their daughter, Beryl, was born in March 1954 at Moody Air Force Base. When husband Ces was studying at Florida State University in Tallahassee, she worked as secretary to Millard Caldwell, former Governor of Florida until sent for by her father in England who was sick and wished to see her and the baby before he died. On her return to the States a few months later she worked as a secretary at the University of Florida where her husband was a student. When her husband's tour of duty in the Air Force finished, he found work in Thomasville, Georgia and she worked as a Court Reporter in the Court House in Thomasville. Joyce became a United States citizen on October 6, 1958 in Albany, Georgia. She worked as a secretary in the U.S. Department of Agriculture Market News, in Thomasville, Georgia, retiring from there after 22 years. She later worked for the State of Georgia. At age 55 she became a long-distance runner, winning many 5, 10 and 15K races in her age group, and 2 mini-marathons when 60. She was an active member of St. Thomas' Episcopal Church in Thomasville, Georgia from 1957 to date. Her 23 yr. old grandson lives with his parents Larry and Beryl Westlake in Lakeland, Florida. Her husband Ces spent his last nine years as a patient in Skilled Nursing in the Presbyterian Home in Quitman, Georgia where he died on April 5, 2004. She was Secretary-Treasurer of the Thomasville Running Club, Secretary-Treasurer of NARFE (National Association of Retired Federal Employees) in Thomasville, served as Auxiliary President of T.L. Spence American Legion Post 31 in Thomasville. Member of Tallahassee Chapter of National Secretaries Association (International). Enjoys gardening, knitting, and reading. In print: wrote 2 pages of Professor Ray Barfield's book, 'Listening to Radio 1920-1950'.

Printed in Great Britain
by Amazon.co.uk, Ltd.,
Marston Gate.